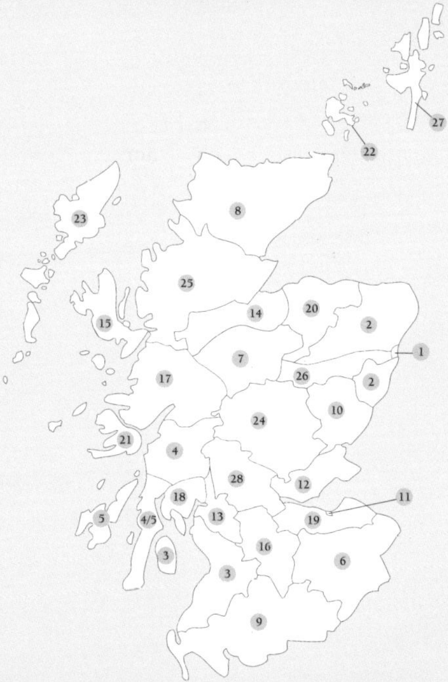

1. Aberdeen
2. Aberdeenshir
3. Arran & Ayrs
4. Argyll
5. Southern Argyll
6. The Borders
7. The Cairngorms
8. Caithness & Sutherland
9. Dumfries and Galloway
10. Dundee & Angus
11. Edinburgh
12. Fife, Kinross & Clackmannan
13. Glasgow
14. Inverness

19. The Lothians
20. Moray
21. Mull & Iona
22. Orkney
23. The Outer Hebrides
24. Perthshire
25. Ross & Cromarty
26. Royal Deeside
27. Shetland
28. Stirling & The Trossachs

The remaining three books, Caledonia, Distinguished Distilleries and Scotland's Mountains, feature locations throughout the country so are not included in the above list.

Ruth Bidgood
May 2015

(from Martin + Jan)

PICTURING SCOTLAND

CALEDONIA

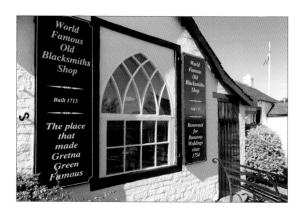

NESS PUBLISHING

2   Dumfries is well described by its soubriquet 'Queen of the South'. This elegant town sits astride the River Nith at its lowest bridging point. There has been a stone bridge on this site since 1432.

CALEDONIA

The structure seen here dates from 1620 as flooding had washed away its predecessor.
It is named Devorgilla Bridge after Devorgilla, the mother of King John Balliol.

Welcome to Caledonia!
('Caledonia', Scotland's Latin-Gaelic name, means 'wooded heights'.)
So named by the Romans, the land we know better as Scotland lies in wait to amaze its visitors with its matchless landscapes, both rural and urban. A TV advertisement states that 'Scotland may surprise you', but this is *such* an understatement: if Scotland doesn't astonish you, ask for your money back! (Not the money for this book, of course, as it will show itself to be such good value that you will more likely want to buy another copy for a friend!)

Scotland's uniqueness lies in the sheer variety of what is to be seen within its relatively compact borders. Think of Scotland as a 'sample patch' specially created to show off virtually every type of scenic wonder the world has to offer. This is the globe in miniature, which on the one hand can offer an almost tropical experience (complete with palm trees) on the right summer day; while on the other, it transports you into an arctic wilderness of tundra and deep, deep snow. In between, there are the mountains and streams, hills and glens, rivers and lochs, cities, towns and villages, forests and farms that routinely bring spectators of the show – visitor and local alike – to a stunned standstill. And there is no 'best bit' of Scotland. To try and turn the different parts of Scotland into a beauty contest would be to miss the point. To one person, the rounded hills and meandering rivers of the Borders will be balm to the soul, while to another the hair-raising majesty of the Cuillins on Skye provides the adrenalin-rush they crave. Each to his/her own!

4

At the southernmost tip of Scotland, in the unspoiled paradise of the Mull of Galloway,   5
stands this lighthouse. Inset: sea thrift is common on Scotland's coast.

The point is that all this variety in one small country makes for a unique concoction of experiences, from one extreme to another.

This book has been eight years in the making, the late fruit of a project to photograph the whole of Scotland in order to publish a regional series of books like this one, but with the difference that they cover the country region by region. With this task essentially achieved, the opportunity has arisen to produce a volume which provides a 'taster' of the entire land. It has been exceptionally difficult to produce, for to represent all of Scotland in about 120 pictures has been challenging indeed. The other books in the series are of similar length and there are 30 of them. This means around 3,000 pictures have been published (out of about 25,000 taken), so to slim that many photographs down to a mere 120 views has been tough. But the good news for the readers of *Caledonia* is that for every picture that

6   As St Ninian brought the light of Christianity to Alba in the 390s, here we have a symbolic sunrise over the Isle of Whithorn, where he established the first (known) church in Scotland.

particularly appeals, you can go on to find a whole book which unpacks that part of the country in much greater thoroughness.

Scotland may look like a bit of a dot on the world map, but in practice travelling from one end to the other is no mean journey. To go by surface, by the most direct route, from its southernmost tip at the Mull of Galloway to the northernmost outpost of Muckle Flugga on Shetland will entail covering approximately 570 miles by road and a minimum of four ferry crossings. This little book takes you on a much longer version of that journey, as we shall criss-cross the country many times in order to take in every area. The starting point is in Galloway and the direction is of course northwards but, like those meandering Borders' rivers, our progress is indirect, enticed to explore every landscape along the way.

Kirkcudbright, Galloway, is a town of many colours, both natural and painted. Artistically, it is re-establishing itself as a centre for arts and crafts, following its earlier period as an artists' colony.

8   Typical Dumfriesshire countryside: a lovely winter scene in upper Annandale, in the north of the county. The hills around here rise to as much as 800m/2624ft.

The magnificent Drumlanrig Castle is constructed from distinctive pinkish sandstone. 9
It was commissioned in 1691 by William Douglas, the first Duke of Queensberry.

10 Now to the Borders, domain of the River Tweed, and Scott's View, north of St Boswells. From the curve of the river to the Eildon Hills, it's not hard to understand why this was Sir Walter Scott's

favourite scene. He designed and built his magnificent home, Abbotsford which overlooks the Tweed between Galashiels and Melrose. Abbotsford is open to the public.

12 Peebles benefits from an idyllic setting and even on a winter night can provide a striking image, with the floodlit Old Parish Church standing tall above the fast-flowing River Tweed.

Turning now to Kelso, the War Memorial gardens provide a lovely foreground to the remains 13
of Kelso Abbey. One of the Borders 'big four' abbeys, Kelso's ruins are very impressive.

14 Robert Burns, Scotland's Bard, was born in Alloway (just south of Ayr) on 25th January 1759 in this cottage. He lived much of his life in Ayrshire, later moving to Dumfries where he died in 1796.

Built on the Ayrshire coast, Culzean is undoubtedly one of Scotland's finest castles. It has developed **15** via a well-trodden path from functional fortification to the neoclassical mansion seen here.

16 The mountainous Isle of Arran is known as 'Scotland in miniature'. Even as you disembark from the ferry, the sight of Goatfell, its highest peak at 874m/2866ft, draws the eye.

Machrie Moor is the epicentre of ancient activity on Arran where a network of sites speaks of huge 17 effort over many centuries. This trio of stones forms the most dramatic grouping.

18 New Lanark Mills, a World Heritage site, grew from a mill into a model industrial community. As this picture shows, it is set deep in the valley where it could exploit the power of the River Clyde.

A mile or so upstream from New Lanark are the majestic Corra Linn Falls. This 27m/90ft waterfall **19** was immortalised in poetry by Wordsworth as 'the Clyde's most majestic daughter'.

20 Some miles to the south stands Tinto Hill in all its considerable glory. Although not the highest at 707m/2319ft, it is Lanarkshire's most prominent and impressive hill, especially from the east.

Over in West Lothian, The Forth Railway Bridge, begun in 1883 and opened in 1890, is seen here **21** from South Queensferry in a view that gives a good sense of its structural complexity.

22 The Pentland Hills rise to the south of Edinburgh in Midlothian. Several reservoirs have been created in the folds of these hills. Glencorse Reservoir is a particularly lovely sight.

East Lothian boasts many pretty villages. Yester Parish Church, Gifford, can be glimpsed through 23 this array of autumn colours. The village takes its name from the Giffords of Yester Castle.

24 And so to Edinburgh: from way up high in the Scott Monument, the view west takes in the National Gallery of Scotland (centre), above which stands Edinburgh Castle on its rock, from where . . .

. . . we see the opposite scene, with the New Town on the left, the Scott Monument in the centre, **25** Waverley Station to its right and Calton Hill beyond, topped by the Nelson Monument.

26 The Royal Mile runs from the castle to the magnificent Baroque Palace of Holyroodhouse.
    Begun in 1503 by James IV, today it remains the official residence of the Royal Family in Scotland.

Calton Hill provides an ideal vantage point from which to see the city, especially when sunset silhouettes **27** the skyline. On the right is a memorial to the Scottish philosopher Dugald Stewart (1753–1828).

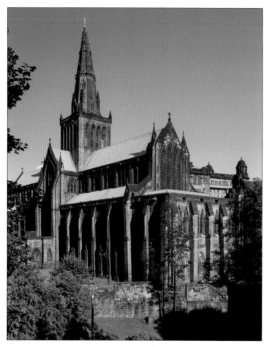

28 Left: from capital city to largest city, this is Glasgow Cathedral. Right: chapel dedicated to St Mungo, Glasgow's founder, in the extensive and atmospheric undercroft of Glasgow Cathedral.

George Square is right at the heart of the city and was laid out in 1801. Glasgow's magnificent City **29** Chambers, built from 1883 to 1888 in the Italian Renaissance style, stand at the far end.

30 The 140m Clyde Arc or 'Squinty' Bridge frames the Finnieston Crane and joins Finnieston on the north bank with Pacific Quay on the south. The bridge is built on the skew, hence the 'squinty' nickname.

Designed by Glasgow's greatest architect Charles Rennie Mackintosh in 1901 (but only built **31** in the 1990s), the House for an Art Lover is in Bellahouston Park on the south side of the city.

32 Situated north-west of Glasgow, Loch Lomond is, by area, Scotland's largest inland loch. This picture is at Tarbet, where the loch narrows and begins to be hemmed in by the surrounding hills.

West of Loch Lomond are the Arrochar Alps. Ben Arthur, usually known as The Cobbler, is their **33** most distinctive mountain at 884m/2900ft. It stands above the village of Arrochar.

34 The town of Rothesay on the Isle of Bute is home to Scotland's only castle that can boast a circular curtain wall, part of which is seen here. Bute is one of Scotland's favourite holiday islands.

The sea lochs either side of the island are known as the Kyles of Bute. The road that navigates this area has been described as 'the best scenic drive in Scotland' – fair comment on a day like this.

36 Further south in Argyll at the head of the Kintyre peninsula is Tarbert, an attractive town and harbour which can look as enchanting by night as by day.

Left: the Argyll island of Islay is famous for its eight distilleries. This is a cameo of Bruichladdich **37** Distillery. Right: on neighbouring Jura, Beinn Shiantaidh, 757m/2477ft, is one of the three 'Paps'.

38 In central Argyll, this is the beautiful town of Inveraray, seen here from the hill of Duniquaich. The dawn light is just catching the towers of Inveraray Castle, bottom right.

The Kilmartin area is rich in ancient sites and artefacts. This is one of the Temple Wood stone circles. **39**
Right: continuing north, Arduaine Garden is one of Argyll's finest.

40 Oban is Argyll's largest town and a major port for ferries to the Hebrides. In this evening scene, McCaig's Tower is floodlit on the hillside and the Mull ferry is berthed for the night.

Kilchurn Castle, built by Sir Colin Campbell of Glenorchy c.1550, stands on the edge of Loch Awe **41** amid some of Argyll's most beautiful mountain scenery.

42 Moving now to the Isle of Mull, this is the delightful port of Tobermory, one of Scotland's, let alone Mull's, most iconic views. The cruise ship *Hebridean Princess* is berthed on the right.

Mull is a mountainous island and Ben More its highest peak at 966m/3169ft. This is the view **43** north-west from its summit, looking down on Loch na Keal and the island of Eorsa.

44 Mull also has a dramatic coastline, one of its most impressive features being the Carsaig Arches on the south coast. They were formed by the sea when sea levels were higher.

The small but wonderful island of Iona lies just off Mull's most westerly point. Pilgrims come from 45 all over the world to visit Iona Abbey, founded by St Columba in 563AD.

46 Now to central Scotland and Stirling Castle. Here we see the Queen Anne Garden with the Renaissance Palace (home of the newly re-created 'Stirling Heads') beyond and the Great Hall to the right.

Stirling District includes The Trossachs, famous for its scenic views, probably the best of which is 47 the westerly one from the summit of Ben A'an down the length of Loch Katrine.

48 Further north in Stirling District, beautifully located Killin is where the Falls of Dochart cascade through the village. There is much more to see in Killin, including views down Loch Tay.

In central Scotland, an exciting new development in Falkirk: *The Kelpies*, sculpted by Andy Scott, **49** tower a colossal 30m/98ft above the Forth & Clyde canal and form the focus of The Helix.

50 From Falkirk to Fife, and Culross, one of the most remarkable villages in Scotland for the way in which it has left us with a time capsule from the 16th/17th centuries, the period in which it developed.

Also in Fife, Falkland is another place where time has stood still. This is the 'classic' view of Falkland **51**
Palace, a castle transformed by James IV and James V into the Renaissance palace we see today.

52 The East Neuk of Fife is best known for its famously pretty coastal panoramas. St Monans' harbour is backed by uniformly quaint cottages and exemplifies several such port villages.

Historically, St Andrews is one of the most important places in Scotland. Its cathedral (in the **53** foreground) was the country's largest and its university is Scotland's oldest, founded in 1413.

54 Dundee, Scotland's fourth city, stands proudly on the north bank of the Firth of Tay. Caird Hall in City Square is Dundee's principal concert hall. Its foundation stone was laid in 1914.

The county of Angus contains no less than 40% of Scotland's Class 1 agricultural land and 28% of **55** Scotland's potatoes are grown here. This rural view near Brechin sums up its farming heartland.

56 Glamis Castle, near Forfar, is undoubtedly one of Scotland's finest. As the ancestral home of the Earls of Strathmore, it has witnessed more than 600 years of the nation's history.

Lunan Bay is a perfect spot on the Angus coast. This southwards view from above the bay presents **57** the whole glorious two-mile vista that stretches down to Eathie Haven.

58 A classic view of the Fair City of Perth and the River Tay, looking north from Queen's Bridge towards Perth Bridge, built in 1766 by John Smeaton and widened in 1869 by A.D. Stewart.

Perthshire includes the historic county of Kinross-shire, a large part of which is occupied by Loch Leven. **59**
Mary, Queen of Scots, was imprisoned in the castle (right of picture) on an island in the loch.

60 This scene is quintessential highland Perthshire. From above Kinloch Rannoch, Dunalastair Water lies below Schiehallion, 1083m/3553ft, arguably Perthshire's finest mountain.

Blair Castle, in Blair Atholl, is the HQ of Europe's last remaining private army, the Atholl Highlanders. **61**
They are seen here parading at the annual Atholl Gathering in the castle grounds.

62 Moving over to Lochaber, Buachaille Etive Mor, 1021m/3350ft, is gatekeeper of the south-eastern
approach to Glen Coe. The cover picture includes the southern end of this mountain.

Towering above Fort William is Ben Nevis, Britain's highest mountain at 1344m/4406ft. **63**
This picture shows its fearsome north face in the last light of a winter afternoon.

64 Another of Lochaber's iconic scenes is Glenfinnan, where Bonnie Prince Charlie raised his standard and gathered support in 1745. The monument at the head of Loch Shiel commemorates this event.

In northern Lochaber, a road less travelled twists its way to the shores of Loch Quoich en route to its **65** terminus at Kinloch Hourn. Rhododendrons and whin (gorse) in flower show it is early summer.

66 Over the sea (or bridge!) to the Isle of Skye, where Elgol is blessed with one of the most spectacular and perfect views anywhere. The Cuillin Ridge rises beyond Loch Scaviag in this spring view.

Seals can be seen in many places along Skye's coast. Here a group of common seals take it easy in the June sunshine by Loch Scavaig. 67

68 Skye specialises in formidable landscapes. Here on the Trotternish Ridge are many basalt pinnacles, the best known being the 50m/165ft Old Man of Storr, on the right of the picture.

Dunvegan Castle in the north-west of Skye has been continuously owned by the MacLeod family for **69** very nearly eight centuries. Strategically located, it is also of great architectural importance.

70 About 200 miles east of Skye, Aberdeen is Scotland's third-largest city. Union Terrace Gardens provide a tranquil, recreational space in the midst of the city's bustle.

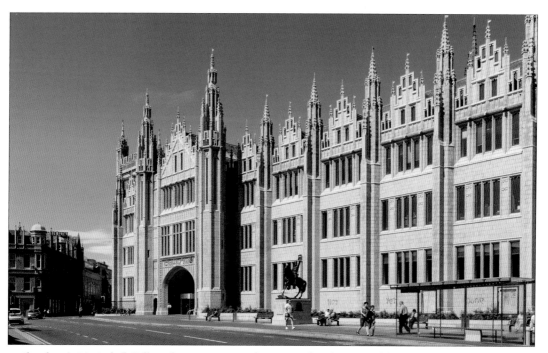

Aberdeen's Marischal College fronts onto Broad Street and is the second-largest granite building in 71 the world. It has recently undergone major renovation and consequently looks superb.

72 Outside the city, Aberdeenshire's hinterland is largely agricultural. The lowland part of its rural landscape is typified in this panorama from Dunnideer hill fort near the town of Insch.

Aberdeenshire has a long coastline with many ports and resorts, a good example being Stonehaven. **73**
The harbour is the historic focus of the town, the first breakwater being built in the 1500s.

74 When it comes to castles, Aberdeenshire has an embarrassment of riches! The most 'fairytale' of all, Craigievar, is a particularly fine sight having recently been restored using traditional limewash.

Gardens are abundant too. Superb Pitmedden Garden near Ellon was originally laid out in 1675 by **75** Sir Alexander Seton and recreated in the 1950s by the National Trust for Scotland.

76 Royal Deeside is a very special part of Aberdeenshire. For many, the River Dee is Scotland's loveliest, a sentiment affirmed by this stretch of its upper reaches near Inverey.

Balmoral Castle, the ultimate symbol of what put the 'Royal' into Deeside. Queen Victoria and Prince Albert purchased Balmoral in 1852 and built this castle which replaced the original structure.

78 The Deeside village of Braemar is famous for the annual Braemar Gathering, always held on the first Saturday in September. It is a magnificent pageant of marching bands and highland games.

Upper Deeside provides this dramatic long-distance view of A'Chioch crags on the eastern edge of **79**
Beinn a'Bhuird (1197m/3927ft), seen from Inverey.

80 East of Aberdeenshire lies the county of Moray, through which flows the River Spey. This precariously taken view from above Telford's bridge at Craigellachie shows Speyside at its summer best.

The remains of Elgin Cathedral, viewed from the west end. Its many outstanding features include **81** the country's finest octagonal chapter house, partly visible on the left.

82 Lossiemouth is on the Moray Firth coast just north of Elgin. From a cave underneath the lighthouse on its west beach, a mid-summer sunrise was captured at about 4.00am.

No book that illustrates Scotland would be complete without mention of whisky and a picture of a distillery. Dating back to 1786, Strathisla Distillery in Keith is perhaps the prettiest.

84 Moray extends into the Cairngorms and it is to this unique mountain range we now turn. It is Britain's largest area of arctic mountain landscape and includes five peaks over 4000ft/1220m.

In the western Cairngorms, Glen Feshie is a long, wild and glorious glen that is not greatly visited, **85**
but well rewards the walk of four miles each way to enjoy this magical vista.

86 The Cairngorms are home to 25% of Britain's endangered birds, animals and plants. Among its rare birds are the capercaillie (left), ptarmigan (upper right) and osprey (lower right).

The Cairngorms in winter mode again; a few tiny figures give scale to the scene. In the distance and miles away to the south, Cairn Toul (1291m/4236ft) breaks through the clouds.

88 Inverness, capital of the Highlands, is north of the Cairngorms and situated on the fast-flowing River Ness at the head of the Great Glen. Inverness Castle was built from 1833 to 1836.

On the moors east of Inverness lies Culloden Battlefield, one of Scotland's most important historical sites. A piper and 'soldier' attend the annual service of remembrance at the commemorative cairn.

90 Urquhart Castle is imposingly situated on the shores of Loch Ness near the village of Drumnadrochit. Its origins as a fortress go back possibly as far as the Iron Age.

Now we go north of the Great Glen to the mountains around famous Glen Affric, about 30 miles **91** south-west of Inverness and one of the most beautiful glens in Scotland.

92 The region north of Inverness is Ross & Cromarty. The eastern part is known as the Black Isle and is the location of the historic county town of Cromarty which juts out into the Cromarty Firth.

Over in Wester Ross is one of Scotland's best mountain panoramas. The view looks east across **93** Loch Torridon towards the Torridon and Achnashellach mountains.

94 Also in Wester Ross, Eilean Donan Castle stands on Loch Duich about seven miles east of Kyle of Lochalsh. The present-day castle was rebuilt from 1912 to 1932.

East of Loch Maree, mighty Slioch (981m/3218ft) is captured on a January evening, showing off a **95** touch of 'Alpenglow' on its full covering of snow. Slioch is usually climbed from Kinlochewe.

96 On the Isle of Lewis in the Outer Hebrides is one of Scotland's most extensive Neolithic sites. This is the main grouping of stones at Calanais (Calanais 1), work on which began around 2900BC.

Harris is the most mountainous part of the Outer Hebrides. The Harris hills are seen here from part of Luskentyre's wonderful beach on South Harris.

98 Cross over to North Uist and another world awaits: seen here from Blashaval, it's a case of water, water everywhere! Here and there, outcrops of rocky hills add relief to the scene.

Barra is one of the southerly islands of the Outer Hebrides. Its principal village is Castlebay, where the ferry *Lord of the Isles* has just docked after its voyage of almost five hours from Oban.

100 The northernmost part of the Scottish mainland is Caithness & Sutherland. This is Dornoch, Sutherland's delightful county town, religious and administrative centre of Sutherland for 800 years.

Sutherland's mountains are a class apart. A wind-blown pine tree provides the perfect framing for **101** Quinag, with its Spidean Coinich summit on the left and Sail Garbh summit to its right.

102 If there were a prize for the most 'fairytale' castle in Scotland, Dunrobin could well be the winner. Although it goes back to the 13th century, what is seen today dates to the mid 1800s.

At Durness, on the north coast of Sutherland, is the amazing Smoo Cave, complete with this waterfall **103** cascading through the roof. Boat rides into the depths of the cavern are available for visitors.

104 Sailing to Orkney from Scrabster provides a spectacular introduction to the islands thanks to the dramatic Hoy coast, the most notable feature of which is the 137m/449ft Old Man of Hoy.

The panorama from Wideford Hill west of Kirkwall gives a wonderful impression of Orkney's pattern **105** of islands. Visible are Gairsay, Wyre, Rousay, Egilsay and, on the horizon, Westray.

106 The Ring of Brodgar is Orkney's largest stone circle and part of the Heart of Neolithic Orkney World Heritage Site, which also includes Maeshowe, the Stones of Stenness and Skara Brae.

St Magnus Cathedral has stood in Kirkwall for more than 800 years. Building began in 1137 under **107** Rognvald, nephew of St Magnus. Even at night, the lovely colour of its sandstone is discernible.

108 And so to Shetland, a landscape which is dominated by the many incursions of great sea lochs and deep bays (known as 'voes'), such as here at Whiteness on the western side of Mainland.

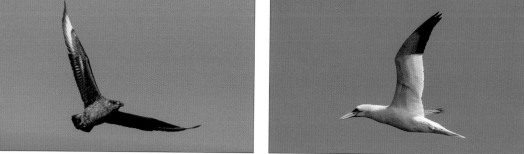

Top left: you can't visit Shetland and not see ponies! Top right: wool is an important part of the **109** Shetland economy. Lower left: great skua, known locally as the 'bonxie'. Lower right: gannet.

110 Shetland scores highly in the spectacular coast stakes, nowhere more so than at Eshaness.
On stormy days it is dangerous to go near the cliff edge as sizeable rocks can be thrown up by the sea.

Journey's end: Hermaness Hill on the island of Unst is home to thousands of Puffins. **111**
And from here, look over to Muckle Flugga and its lighthouse, seen on the back cover.

Published 2015 by Ness Publishing, 47 Academy Street, Elgin, Moray, IV30 1LR
Phone 01343 549663 www.nesspublishing.co.uk
All photographs © Colin and Eithne Nutt except p.4 © Charlie Phillips; p.86 (all) © Mark Hicken
Text © Colin Nutt
ISBN 978-1-906549-29-9

Front cover: Buachaille Etive Beag and Buachaille Etive Mor from Glen Etive; p.1: The Old Blacksmith's Shop, Gretna Green; p.4: red squirrel; this page: Highland Cattle in Sutherland; back cover: Muckle Flugga, Shetland

For further information about *Picturing Scotland* resources, please see overleaf. > > > >

Photographic prints

If you have enjoyed the photographs in this book and would like prints of these or others from our extensive (25,000 images) photo library, please contact us with your request.

Colin and Eithne Nutt at Ness Publishing, 47 Academy Street, Elgin, Moray, IV30 1LR
Phone 01343 549663 www.nesspublishing.co.uk for further details